A JOURNEY THROUGH THOUGHT

A LOOK AT FAMILY, LIFE AND NEGRITUDE THROUGH QUOTES,
POEMS AND SHORT STORIES

REV. DR. TAHLIB MCMICHEAUX

WITH CONTRIBUTIONS BY:

MCMICHEAUX AND JANELLE MCMICHEAUX

A Journey Through Thought
A Look at Family, Life and Negritude
Through Quotes, Poems and Short Stories

For information, contact : BTLifecoaching@gmail.com
Cover design by : https://www.fiverr.com/rebecacovers
ISBN: 978-1721985746

First Edition: July 2018

10 9 8 7 6 5 4 3 2 1

ACKNOWLEDGEMENTS

Hello, my friends.

As you can see, I am at it again, only this time with a compilation of quotes, poems, and short stories. Since my first book and workshop that followed, I have had many requests and inquiries about my next writing project. I know it has been a while, but here it is, and I pray you will savor every word written, allowing them to guide you to your deepest thoughts, challenge your traditions and cultural views, and in the end, broaden your scope of understanding. We are only limited by the confines of our thoughts and imagination.

I would like to thank God for giving me the courage to creatively do something different in this book. I have been a non-traditionalist for as long as I can remember. For years, all I wanted was to fit in and be accepted by the norm, but once I stopped fighting with being unique and realizing this was not a curse but a gift, I gave myself the latitude to walk in the truth of my unique creative ability and from that point on I have never looked back. I believe there are so many people in the world who are still wrestling with their unique and unconventional characteristics, people who are unable to free the creative energies within because they are spending so much time trying to conform. This book is for those who are ready to break out of the cocoon of normality and experience the freedom of being you in all of its expressed creativeness. There is an old saying, Let go and let God.

I would like to thank my wife, Patricia McMicheaux, for her countless hours of proofreading until her eyes were crossed and for the many times she sacrificed for the sake of reading one more paper. There were many days when I experienced surges of creativity while taking long walks or sitting in the break room, having only a wrinkled piece of paper to jot my notes on. My wife mastered the skill of decoding, in the most literal sense of the word, for she took my scribble, often written on anything I could find with an empty space, and translated it into something legible and even profound.

There is one person who encouraged me throughout this entire process, and I would be remiss if I did not acknowledge her support emotionally,

spiritually, and creatively. Sharon Harris is my editor, and her gentle spirit and kind words became my greatest inspiration. She made the journey an incredible experience that I plan to replicate with future projects.

I would like to thank my two daughters, Naheemah McMicheaux and Janelle McMicheaux, and my son, Tahlib McMicheaux, for providing me with some of the greatest learning experiences in my life through parenting them as children. I will be forever grateful for all they have taught me as I watched them blossom into productive, creative, and responsible human beings. I am honored to know that however minute the part I played was in their growth and development, I was a contributor.

I am also grateful to my daughters for giving me the loves of my life, my five grandbabies: Alexander, NaMia, Jennifer, Jackson, and Jordan. They bring joy in the mere thought of their existence, and I smile at the thought that my favorite people in the world call me papa.

To those whom I have not named in this acknowledgment, I would like to thank you for your support, encouragement, kind words, and for just believing in me, much love.

Rev. Dr. Tahlib McMicheaux

ABOUT THE AUTHOR

Dr. Tahlib McMicheaux attended El Camino College, Los Angeles City College, College of the Desert, California Baptist College, Southern Christian Bible College, and Sacramento Theological Seminary where he graduated *magna cum laude*. He holds a Doctorate and Master's Degree in Theology. He is a pastor/teacher and a National Certified Life Coach, and he is dean of the Sacramento Theological Seminary. Dr. McMicheaux is a Ronald E. McNair Scholar and is also listed in the *Who's Who Among Students in American Universities and Colleges*, 1994-1995.

He is the founder of Igniting the Fire Movement--The Changing Face of Evangelism, and he is one of Coachella Valley's distinguished community advocates – a seasoned pastor/teacher and life coach. He is a recognized leader in pastoral circles for his in-depth teachings and thought-provoking, life-changing sermons. His workshops are equally stimulating and challenging.

Widely viewed as a visionary, his creative energy has been sought after by congress, governors, and local elected officials. As a pastor and community leader, he is one of a select few community advocates who have been asked to work with communities of all ethnic backgrounds in and around the Southern California area.

As a community activist Dr. McMicheaux has been an advocate for the disenfranchised and under-represented in America and throughout our local communities for over 25 years, speaking at rallies, town halls, and, of course, churches. He was called on to speak at one of the most prestigious colleges in New York, addressing the state of homelessness in the Coachella Valley.

Dr. McMicheaux's journey through life can be described in one word—tenacious. Born with two strikes—a learning disability called dyslexia and being a person of color—he chose to defy the odds. With over thirty awards and certificates recognizing and honoring his work as a community leader and activist, you can see by his many accomplishments that such barriers were only momentary obstacles which he chose to rise above. When asked about these accomplishments he will say his work is just beginning. I celebrate the man who wrote this book because he happens to be my husband and best friend.

Patricia McMicheaux

DEDICATION

This book is dedicated to my ancestors, those people in my life who paved the way for me to be where I am, for their dedication and commitment and struggle through the difficult times they lived in, braving each day in hopes that the next generation would be able to get one step closer to the freedom they never experienced.

I am grateful to know that behind me is a legacy of strength, and in front of me is the history I will leave for my grandchildren and theirs to come. I am grateful for Mama Celeste, my great-grandmother, whom I vaguely recall. Without her I would not have had the experiences I so fondly remember with my grandmother, Bernice Kemp, and the person she married, Charlie Kemp, who was the other half of the union that gave life to my mother, Charlene Leola Kemp. This is my maternal gratitude.

My gratitude on my paternal side is to my two uncles who spoke into my life while they were alive and continue to direct me after joining the council of elders that watches over me. To all the elders who have so greatly impacted my life in so many ways, I thank God for the time I was able to journey with you.

Rev. Dr. Tahlib McMicheaux

FORWARD

Many books have been written, some for information, some for inspiration, and some for self-promotion. The author of this book is a man of God and could only have the best interest of the reader at heart. I have known Dr. McMicheaux for over 25 years, and from the first time I met him, I felt that I wanted to know him better and develop a relationship with him. No one who has ever had the pleasure of meeting or conversing with Dr. McMicheaux can walk away with anything but the feeling that they have met a person who has a connection with a higher power as well as their best interest at heart. When speaking with him one realizes they have his undivided attention.

I had the honor and privilege of spending the entire month of September 2016, with Dr. McMicheaux and his beautiful wife, Patricia, as they walked the Cross from his church in Desert Hot Springs, California, through the streets of Southern California, Los Angeles County, and finally on the streets of downtown Sacramento, California. He and Patricia walked those streets without a book or an agenda, but only the desire to learn about the people they encountered and using their stories to grasp a better understanding of their condition and how it connects to our relationship with God. I realized that this is something he is doing at all times. In furthering that connection, Dr. McMicheaux has written this book to inspire and to challenge the reader to journey into the world of thought in the hopes that they might elevate their consciousness to a different level of understanding and connection.

In closing, I have come to realize over my lifetime that there are two kinds of Christians, those who consider themselves

Christians because they attend a Christian church and those who consider themselves Christians because they follow the tenets exemplified by Christ in the Bible, and for the latter, those readers will find a true connection with Dr. Tahlib McMicheaux's words.

Rudolpho Alegria, M.D.

INTRODUCTION

In many ways, writers are exhibitionist who bare themselves to the bone to tell a story for their audience. I, too, have agreed to become an exhibitionist, uncovering my history, exposing family skeletons, and revealing my personal thoughts on how it feels to be a person of color in America. I am an idealist who believes that at the core of every human being there is some goodness, and at the core of every unjust system there is some hope.

I believe this book will raise questions in the minds and hearts of those who dare to be independent thinkers. When you think about racial equality, do you have a question mark in the back of your thoughts? When you think of justice in America, do you picture the scales as being balanced or unbalanced? When you think of civil rights, do you see yourself as being liberated or still restricted? The answer to this last question will determine, in many cases, your vantage- or disadvantage-point in America. This book, in its simplicity, will challenge you to think beyond your advantage or disadvantage. This small, powerful book of few words touches on recovery, addiction, growth, healing, and a vision to reach nations.

I originally wrote this book as a catharsis to allow myself a means to process through the many "why" questions I found myself asking daily. It seemed for many of my "whys," no one had the answers. However, as I started writing, I realized the message was larger than my own self-serving need to know why, for there are many others asking the same questions, and they only need a little stimulation to find the answers to the questions within themselves.

This book also captures a unique perspective because before each quote, poem, and story, I give the reader an insight into the inspiration that spurred my writing about a very delicate and sensitive moment in my life. This way the reader does not have to spend time guessing but thinking.

The truth is we have a nation to build, and at the end of the day we need each other to change the laws, communities, cities, and individuals. I believe this book will challenge the reader to reconnect with the greater good of all humanity.

Rev. Dr. Tahlib McMicheaux

CONTENTS

THOUGHTS AND QUOTES

RECOVERY

Preface

I have often shared with my parishioners that God operates in the miraculous and the process. The unfortunate thing about living in a world that wants everything instantaneously is, when we do not receive immediate gratification, we often feel we have failed or God is not on our side. This kind of immediate gratification, when associated with a generation, is often referred to as the "microwave" generation. It appears, at times, that all the generations within our society are now functioning like the microwave generation—meaning no one is willing to go through the process.

From my perspective, it appears this generation is constantly asking God to prove Himself because they have convinced themselves to believe that if God does not show up in their ETA there is no hope. The sad thing about this is not only do we live in a world that has bought into this one-sided philosophy, but many of our faith-based organizations are espousing a similar theology as truth. In some ways they are leading people to believe that God is a God of only the miraculous and not a God of the process. So when we ask why people today are hopeless, maybe it is because many have lost sight of a balanced God that is congruent in all circumstances.

When I am in harmony with the process, I am more willing to endure the experience that is transporting me to my next level of consciousness. So what is your perspective on the process, the journey, and life?

Enjoy.

RECOVERY

Recovery is a process, life is a journey,
and happiness is a decision.

WHEN IS THEN?

Preface

The English language is filled with words that are intriguing, expressive, and even stimulating. These words help us describe, create, and share ideas, stories, and thoughts. However, not all the words in the English language are as captivating as others, such as the word "then." This adverb is often only used to support a thought and almost never used to create a thought. So my challenge in this piece is to not only create a thought using the word "then," but to allow a story to evolve that supports my desire to use the adverb that is rarely presented as the key word to create a thought.

The journey which gave me a deeper understanding of this subtle adverb came about when I was traveling through the Middle East with a handpicked team of pseudo anthropologist/ sociologist. We were all about two and a half years into our studies and thought we were the next Indiana Joneses of biblical archaeology. Using participant observations, we would conduct a cultural study of Middle Eastern people, and our second goal was to look at how previous civilizations within the culture could have an impact on present and future societies. There was no doubt that our work was cut out for us as we moved from region to region gathering data.

While in the Middle East, our schedule was rigorous, and the work was often laborious, requiring tedious documenting at the end of each day to memorialize the day's events of excavating ancient sites. As anthropologist and sociologist, we were also looking for patterns within the culture that transcended civilizations and documentation of early man.

We found many magnificent traditions within each civilization that had left its mark on past and present cultural groups. However, as I began to research traits and commonalities, I found one trait that appeared to run deeper than culture, tradition, family orientation, and religious association. This trait or commonality was linked to mankind before the first recording of man.

The one trait I found which transcended culture and tradition was man's need to engage in some form of war, creating an atmosphere of violence that would spread from region to region and generation to generation. As I mused over this thought, what became clear to me was that this trait rested at the core of man's inner being and described the nature of man across the globe. I realized this trait was not an isolated trait found only in the Middle East but a reflection of what happens when man's need to dominate supersedes his desire to co-exist peacefully and share resources.

As I cogitated this thought, it became a sad commentary on the existence of human nature that in spite of all the advanced civilizations that have come and gone and which exhibited a sophistication that still perplexes modern minds today, there has never been a time in history when man did not use violence and force as a means of dominance. In all of this world's historical splendor, there has almost never been a time, nor a place, where war and violence have not been a major influence on each society, past and present.

The Middle East merely became the impetus for me to envisage a larger trait that impacts man across the globe. As I traveled through the Middle East looking for connections that transcended beliefs, cultures, and traditions, my greatest find was, indeed, my saddest find, which was man's inability to control his insatiable desire to engage in war and violence. This find transcends time, culture, tradition, and religious beliefs, for wherever man is found across the globe, there you can find the aftermath of war and violence. As I grasped the gravity of this find, my heart began to fill with dismay, for if this trait reflects man's past and present behavior, what does it tell us about our future? When is then?

Enjoy.

WHEN IS THEN?

Then will I awaken from the dreams of life which held me
bound to the thoughts of man.

When is then?

SEE THE DISTRACTION?

Preface

Every year as pastor, I would come up with a saying to inspire the church members to go deeper in their spiritual development. I generally presented these little sayings around January so the members could reflect on them throughout the course of the year. Most of the time I knew when the saying was meaningful because it resonated with the developments in my life. This one particular year it was no different.

This one year I was working on finishing my doctorate degree and feeling like I could not read another book or write another paper. As a matter of fact, at the apex of my academic journey, I felt like I was ready to jump out of a plane without a parachute. My academic studies had climaxed with timelines, impatient professors, overlooked typographical errors, and sleep deprivation. In my personal life, it seemed like time had halted communication challenges, family issues, overdue bills, unemployment, and health challenges. And on top of all this, I want you to remember that during these challenges I still had a growing church with a flock that looked forward to receiving a substantive message each Sunday, which meant that not only did I have to research information for my dissertation, but I also had to research information for the upcoming Sunday service.

At this point in my life, everything seemed cloudy and out of focus. Have you ever reached a point in your life where you were so close to a breakthrough that you could feel it on one hand but on another level nothing seemed obtainable? With only a few chapters to go in completing my dissertation, I seriously entertained thoughts of saying enough. I felt challenged and burdened from the pulpit to the home I shared with my wife. The interesting thing about unhappiness is it does not discriminate. It seemed the things I loved and enjoyed the most had turned into devices of irritation upon sight, thought, or sound. The more I grappled with this feeling the more irritated I became until I was unable to mask my unhappiness with family, friends, and wife. It was at this point I realized that desperate times needed desperate measures. I have a plaque hanging in my office that reads, "When life gets too hard to stand, kneel." So I headed down to the church to do what I had suggested to so many over my years of pastoring—kneel, release, and rise anew.

Now I know I could have spoken to Him in the house or in the car or even in the parking lot of the church. I knew I needed His attention, and what better place to demand His attention than in the Tabernacle of Meeting. I found myself feeling like I had so much to say and could not wait to say it as I entered the building from a starlit parking lot, attempting to make my way down a long corridor which led to the sanctuary. Now inside, I found myself blinded by an abyss of darkness, my first distraction to prevent me from reaching my destination. Once I positioned myself at the entrance of the sanctuary, I was challenged by my inability to find the light switch which was, by the way, my second distraction.

My third distraction was the things within the darkness which could cause me to stumble. I found it peculiar to think that the pews which had served the congregation faithfully for so many years had now become one of my greatest distractions in the dark that could prevent me from reaching my blessings. So in order to accomplish my desired task, I knew I needed to see the distraction while focusing on the blessing to benefit from the outcome. So my question to you is, "How many times in your life have those things which are so familiar become a distraction that takes your attention away from your destination?"

Enjoy.

10

SEE THE DISTRACTION?

See the distraction, but focus on the blessings.

THE SOUL

Preface

Some thoughts are worthy of rethinking and this is one of them. An unknown author once wrote, "Anything written is twice thought." For this reason, I must rethink to formulate the thought, and then I must memorize the thought on paper, capturing the very essence of my idea for generations to rethink.

While watching Oprah Winfrey's Super Soul Sunday, Oprah Winfrey asked the person she was interviewing this question, "What is the Soul?" Well, as I ruminated over this question, seeking an answer to appease the inner wrestling that I was experiencing, God gave me this.

Enjoy.

THE SOUL

What is the soul?

The eternal movement of God's spirit operating in the confinements of human existence.

LIVE WHAT YOU PREACH

Preface

I came up with this saying to challenge my ministers and keep them focused on their journey. I often remind them of this quote before our meeting and just before we close our meeting. Over the years I have used mantras to help the congregation stay focused on their mission and purpose as believers. This mantra reminds us to "keep it real."

Live What You Preach

Live what you preach.

Preach what you live.

And if you can't live it, don't preach it.

WHEN YOU ARE IN THE WILL OF GOD

Preface

I once worked at a place where I increasingly became tired of pretending I desired to be there day after day. These feelings incited an inner battle that caused me concern over whether I was blowing the witness as a believer because I had become a grumbling, complaining, unhappy person.

I believe the challenge for all believers is to be real with their feelings. But the greatest challenge is to surrender our feelings to the Lord daily, believing that He will give us the strength to overcome our challenges. This is what I believe I received in the spirit that God gave me during my time in prayer as he brought peace to my soul.

Enjoy.

Forgive me God for my momentary decent into the life of Jonah.

WHEN YOU ARE IN THE WILL OF GOD

When you are in the will of God,

You may not be where you want to be.

But if you are in the will of God,

You are where you are supposed to be.

HURT PEOPLE HURT

Preface

I have often wondered why, when I encounter people who are unhappy living with unresolved issues, they seem to have an internal desire to pass on their misery. This has remained an enigma for many years until recently. Sometimes maturity brings clarity to the most baffling situations in life. I believe each human being is given a wellspring straight from the reservoir of the most high. I will refer to this wellspring as living water. (John 7:38 [New King James Version].)

Now, as life experience presents opportunities for doubt, despair, unbelief, resentment, unforgiveness, and anger, these conditions begin to block the ability for the living water to pass through our wellsprings. When this happens, negativity builds up in our well until it becomes toxic. For years, I have said, "Anything that becomes stagnate runs the risk of becoming polluted." Polluted water is vile and virulent and filled with harmful bacteria waiting to attach itself to a new host and then seeking to destroy it from the inside out.

Some might ask, Why would someone be so calculating and pernicious? The answer is simple – because that is the purpose of polluted water. You see, when living water ceases to flow through us, our purpose changes along with our perspective. Yes, without living water passing through us, washing out the negativity and reintroducing belief, hope, determination, resistance, and strength, the end result is a wellspring filled with pollution. Now when people encounter these polluted wellsprings, they often do not notice right away that they are contaminated. Sometimes these polluted

19

wells are very attractive on the outside, deceiving others into believing that they have living water flowing in and through them, but that is far from the truth. Years of blockage have caused them to become contaminate and lethal. So trusting the outer and not examining the inner, we partake in the pollution of others, becoming infested by their dis-ease. Hence, hurt people spread dis-ease.

Enjoy.

Hurt People Hurt

Hurt people hurt and wounded people spread dis-ease.

THE MELODY OF JOY

Preface

As a music lover it is hard to imagine living in a world without this form of auditory stimulation. Music is such an intrinsic part of our world that it transcends culture, generations, and even religion. Take the bible for example. It is an accumulation of 66 books, 40 authors, and 1189 chapters. The bible was written over a period of 1500 years or from 1400 BC to AD 90, and music was a driving influence from Genesis to Revelations.[1]

Looking at the span of time it took to write the bible, it becomes clear that it was not a coincidence that each book used some form of music as a vital part of its sensory expression. The bible is riddled with references to music, such as melody, song, hymn, instrument, sound, play, blow noise, psalm, harp, lyre, horn, voice and the word music itself,[2] all implying that music had the power to transform the lives of the listeners.

To illustrate the essence of human nature, this piece was reduced down to two emotional polarities, happy and sad. These two operate like the yin and the yang of life's melodies, with everything else existing in between.

The message in this quote is intended to resonate in the heart of every reader: "Life is a choice—choose to live in the expressed melodies that major in joy as opposed to the minors of life that dwell in the dissonance of unhappiness."

Enjoy

---

[1] *How Long Did it Take to Write the Bible?*, April 10, 2018, Got Questions, http://www.gotquestions.org/write-the-Bible.html

[2] *References to Music in the Bible*, April 10, 2018, In Search of Truth, http://www.insearchoftruth.org/music_references.html

THE MELODY OF JOY

When the melody of joy leaves,
it is often replaced with the dissonance of dolefulness.

POEMS

FOLLOW THE LIGHT

Preface

This piece comes out of my spiritual journey seeking God. As a new convert to Christianity, I grappled with staying in the light. I understood how to vacillate between light and darkness. I had done that successfully all my life, but I did not truly understand how to commit myself to the continuous flow of light shining from above—the light that rendered me vulnerable to its presence.

Throughout my life I had followed desire, friends, and the latest craze that caused me to appear as part of the "in" group. I believe through this piece, my journey to salvation became clearer. I was amazed at what God allowed me to see when my eyes were opened, and I began to follow the light.

Enjoy.

FOLLOW THE LIGHT

Ever since man's creation he has been standing in damnation
Not knowing which way is right
He just can't find the light

All he needs is to open his eyes and look to the heavenly
skies
Call out His name and not be ashamed
For it is He who can set you free
Follow the light
Follow the light
Follow the light

I know there will be doubt
What is it all about?
For the man who only feels by touch
Has lost so very much

I called out and It wasn't in vain
The Master heard and spoke my name
He said
Follow the light
Follow the light
Follow the light

GROWTH

Preface

My eldest daughter grew up living in the shadows of her dad who was at that time a community and social activist. As a social activist, I was always reading to expand my knowledge base or reference point. It was not unusual for her to hear her dad debating at a forum or speaking at a workshop somewhere. I decided early on that I would not lower my standards of communication in my home just because my daughter was a child just a few years past being a toddler. So I decided to intellectually stimulate her as we engaged in these daily discussions about school, homework, teachers, and yes, boys.

It did not take long before she started regurgitating the words I used when speaking to her. However, her understanding of her neo-vocabulary could only be described as creative. From the age of 10 to about 13, we engaged in some of the most philosophically moving conversations that I had to silently interpret the meaning of the words she used out of context. I would nod and smile as though the words she used were followed by the mysteries of wisdom itself. Somewhere around 14 years old the vocabulary and the context of the words she had been misusing collided at an intersection of maturity, and this poem emerged out of the intellectual, the philosopher, and the person who was ready to share her voice with the world.

Enjoy.

GROWTH

By

Naheemah McMicheaux

In the beginning
We are a mere seed
In the earth's womb

As growth takes place
We become sprouts
Seeking to find the Sun

As the sun provides us with
The photosynthesis of life's nutrition
We enter the world and see it's many
Changes.

We grow leaves and wait to blossom

Once we blossom we see
The world as it really is
We learn to adapt to its many changes

With every season there is a challenge

Will I succumb to the coldness of winter
Will I shrivel up and die in the heat of summer
Will I live in the past of what once was!
When fall leaves me bare
Will the growth of spring agitate me
to the point of avoidance

I will reach to the heavens
With the determination of life

I will blossom to experience all
That God would have me to
And like all good plants

One day the beauty of what I once was
Will be no more
The green will turn to gold.
That which reached up will start to droop
I will wither caressed by time past
And maybe even question
what it was all about.

Then will I remember my purpose
I will remember the seeds that I set free in the wind
To experience the four seasons over again
And to enter and exit the revolving door of life.

THANKSGIVING DINNER

Preface

This piece was written by my youngest daughter while in middle school just transitioning from elementary school. In her writing she was able to capture the innocence of a person fresh out of elementary school and yet the sophistication in the formation of thought that lends toward the preparation of a budding high school student. This piece reminds me that in all of our lives there was a time of innocence where the world became the greatest classroom we ever sat in with all its poignant lessons.

As you read this piece be reminded of the time of innocence in your life, the excitement and drama within each day of middle school, the youthful exuberance that comes from inexperience and immaturity, the creativity unrefined but desiring to be harnessed and released on the world around you, and the idealism personified that told you the impossible was possible. Sometimes simple is just enough.

Enjoy.

THANKSGIVING DINNER

By

Janelle McMicheaux

Thanksgiving dinner bad and hopeless,
Turkey feasts are sad and blue,
When you stop and try and see
It from the turkeys point of view

Christmas dinners sad and lonely,
Chicken feasts are just bad luck,
When you see it from the viewpoint
Of a chicken and a duck.

Oh how I once loved tuna salad,
Pork and lobsters, lamb chops too,
Till I stopped and looked at dinner
From the dinner point of view.

SHOME

Preface

In the 80s someone created a street drug called Sherm. This highly addictive drug devastated the streets of L. A. and many other minority communities. This drug was so lethal, toxic, and poisonous, it instantaneously transformed the living into the walking dead, filled with elephant tranquilizer and embalming chemicals. Many that tried it never recovered.

Sherm was a quick and cheap high that reduced the "biggest and baddest" on the streets into nothing more than an empty shell with glossy eyes and inaudible sounds that said, "No one is home." I watched friends and family members become strung out on this drug. I walked into the pits of hell to share a loving word from my Sunday text to those who would listen, but for the most part, no one was home.

Sherm was a cheap and quick high and for many their last. I remember during this time there was a lot of talk about meditation and being at peace with yourself. So I borrowed from the word the people were using to meditate on which was "ome" and added an "sh" and came up with the word "shome." "Shome," the meditation of hell that took people into the clutches of death each time they experimented. There are many people who live on the edge—some come back and others become the casualty of being a risk taker. Many brilliant minds were lost during that time of drug-induced meditation.

Enjoy.

Who is "Shome"
Shome is the drug of choice, a habit that compels one to leave all that they know for a ritualistic daily meditation at the altar of addiction.

SHOME

This high I feel
It just can't be for real
My mind has been blown
By a little stick called shome.

O-shome leave me alone

I was just trippen
Slippen and sliding with the gang
Because I thought I could hang

O-shome leave me alone

My friends a gone
And I'm all alone
To deal with a ride
That's been breaking my stride

O-shome leave me alone
I'm going down fast
And I just can't last
They say once you take
You just can't quit

O-shome leave me alone

I just wanted to try
I didn't want to die

O-shome leave me alone
O-shome leave me alone

35

INCONCEIVABLE INNOVATION

Preface

Having spent time lecturing on shame, blame, guilt, and unforgiveness for many years, I have come to the realization that there is a place in human nature when we all experience these feelings to some degree. The only difference is, some choose to live in this state while others fight until they are free of its gripping clutches.

In this piece, I am asking readers to reflect on a moment in their lives when everything seemed to pass them by, and they are left feeling isolated and alone.

For the purposes of this composition, I am going to call this place "Stuck!" Stuck is the place where you are internally screaming for help but externally devoid of the ability to inform others that your outward appearance is nothing more than camouflaged emotions. Stuck is the self-induced state of numbness that justifies being detached from your present state, fearful of your future, and longing to relive your past. Stuck is a place of moving forward while looking backward.

I sympathize with those who are caught in this vicious cycle. Being stuck is not a metaphor; it is a real place that many enter and are not freed until they open their eyes in hopes of a paradise without phobias or fears. One person described being stuck as an inability to move forward emotionally, physically, and spiritually; it was like being stuck in the quick sands of powerlessness, relinquishing all rights of hopefulness while being pulled down into the abyss of nothingness.

This piece was written to challenge readers to examine their focus, past and future.

Enjoy.

INCONCEIVABLE INNOVATION

Must I be shadowed by the past?
The loss of love and the gold grass rises so high
Like memories soaring through time
The metamorphosis of mind and body
I have lived the past that I so regretfully left behind
Now trapped in sophisticated times which I cannot
comprehend
I sit ponder and wait for the past to join me once again.

SHORT STORIES

MY PRAYER TODAY

Preface

My wife and I went to a counselor to see how we could strengthen a couple areas of our marriage. I listened with great interest to what the therapist had to say. She asked probing questions that caused us to think and reflect. She tapped into emotions and feelings that had been repressed, and she listened to us with the intensity of a deaf person hearing sound for the first time, all the while never breaking her gaze. This told us we had her undivided attention.

The guidance we received from her took us through a myriad of emotions that were often exhausting, leaving us speechless at the end of the session. However, I recall one particular session that left a lasting impression on my psyche. She stated, in her coy demeanor, that relationships are about *healing, learning, and growing*. As a thinker, these words caused my light bulb to go on, and I found them intriguing as a skeptic, believing they had no relevance in relation to marriage and especially my marriage.

However, one day I did more than ponder these words. As a believer, I got down on my knees and began to pray, asking God to reveal to me the depth and truth of these words. For some reason, I knew in my spirit that there was a greater truth that I needed to experience, but I just didn't know how to reach it. As a pastor who counseled and directed people to walk in their truth, I felt convicted enough to reexamine my truth. The bible tells us the Holy Spirit will guide us in all truth, but I believe the first truth we are guided through is the truth about ourselves. This is the truth most of us spend a lifetime attempting to avoid because in life we become masters of redirecting the attention from ourselves to others.

Now I must say, be careful what you ask God to reveal to you. God revealed, in no uncertain terms, the truth and depth of these words over the course of a couple of days. As I allowed myself to enter into the process of introspection of **healing, learning, and growing**, I went to a place in my spirit that I had not been before. The first thing that was revealed to me was I had spent a lot of time focusing on my wife's shortcomings and looking for the healing that was needed for her fragile emotional state. I now felt like John, in the book of Revelations who was asked to write what was revealed to him at the height of an awakened subconscious state (Rev 1:19). It was during this time of personal revelation that I saw myself holding a bag and sprinkling the contents outward like fairy dust on all those around me, only to discover that the real contents within my bag were shattered pieces of pottery indicating the state of my brokenness.

No one or thing was off limits to my brokenness. I often wondered why people responded to my presence with indifference, grabbing their umbrellas when I entered the room. They were shielding themselves from the jagged, cutting edges of sharp pottery falling from the sky around me. In my state of denial, completely oblivious of the pain I was forcing others to experience, I told myself that everyone else had a problem that only God could cure, including my wife.

I was now directed to one of the words I had been pondering for some time, **healing**. It dropped down like one of the balls popping out in a lottery machine, only this time the word came alive as God showed me its relevance in all my misguided stubbornness. I felt in my spirit that this was not going to be just another feel-good conviction of the Holy Spirit that I had become so accustomed to experiencing. God showed me that true healing begins with me because I had become a master of redirecting my responsibility of initiating healing in my marriage to my wife. I realized in one stroke of conviction that I had been pointing my index finger outward to avoid looking at the three other fingers pointing back at me. He showed me the disparity between living in broken arrogance and loving in humility.

Standing in the chagrin of my unforgiving heart, I realized I still had two more words to go. At this point, I braced myself for the next word which was *learning*. Still experiencing momentary spurts of fleeting self-righteousness, I wondered what conviction could come from this word. God shared with me that I had learned in some of the greatest institutions of higher learning; I had learned in conferences listening to dynamic speakers; I had learned on the job; all making me a student of learning **about** everything else except myself. In all my life lesson of learning, I had failed to humble myself before my wife to learn her. Not only had I failed to learn from her, I had failed to learn her as a unique, divinely-created human being.

Having earned my master's degree in theology, I realized I had not even earned my Associate of Arts degree in knowing and understanding my wife. I realized I had abandoned learning her when I stopped courting her. It was revealed to me that my most important degree was not the one earned in school but the one earned at home. You see, I have shared over the years in workshops and the pulpit that ministry begins at home. It seems I had forgotten the words I had preached with such fervency. The great thing about God's grace and spousal forgiveness is it is never too late.

Again, standing before God, humbled by the insanity of my thoughtlessness and lack of prioritizing in perspective to the longevity of my marriage, I prepared myself for the next word. At this point, I was reluctantly ready for the last word. I was already convicted and embarrassed by past behaviors that had been revealed to me in the deepest of my spirit. In some ways, I guess you could say, God had opened me up and allowed me to see the truth that I lived to avoid.

The last word was *growing*, and this word revealed to me that all those times I allowed myself to wallow in unforgiveness, lack of trust, and brokenness, I poured salt into the wounds of my marriage. All those times I remained stagnant, dwelling on the past, holding my wife and my marriage captive to the wounded child that had never healed, I stifled the growth and future of our relationship.

You see, anything standing still runs the risk of becoming polluted, and I was starting to stink with the pollution of resentment and stagnation. From this place of self-discovery, I set out to re-learn my wife all over again, realizing that without healing we would not reach growth. I realized for the first time that my marriage had been stifled by my not acknowledging my own faults and shortcomings.

This statement summarizes my journey: When relationships meet the willingness to look within oneself for truth, absent blame, shame, and unforgiveness, there is only one place left for it to go and that is *healing, learning, and growing*. Out of this came my daily prayer for my wife.

Enjoy.

MY PRAYER TODAY

My Prayer Today Is To:

- Learn
- Grow
- Heal

1. My mate has something to **teach** me today. And if I am open, I will hear and learn something from him/her. If I am closed, I will continue to be **resistant, defensive** and **guarded**.

2. My mate can, If I allow him or her to, help me grow to become a better person. A seed is challenged when it attempts to **grow** in unforgiving conditions.

3. **Healing** happens best in a positive environment where mind, body and spirit are connected and filtered through humility.

Today I desire to **learn and grow** and to allow my past wounds to **heal.**

Thank you God for giving me **wisdom** to change the things I can and to expect the things I cannot change as part of my own journey **in learning, growing, and healing**. I am only responsible for me.

Amen.

TWISTED SMILE

Preface

I wrote this piece based on a picture I found while thumbing through a magazine. There were so many different elements to this picture that caught my eyes, causing me to stare, taking in every detail as though I were an artist getting ready to transpose what I was seeing to canvas. I knew within minutes that I had to write about the story found deep within this photo. This picture was my inspiration for the piece called *Twisted Smile*. Now, because there are no other pictures in this book, I decided to attempt to take the reader into the picture I used to write this story without them actually seeing what I viewed with my eyes. My goal is to help the reader open up his or her imagination and see through the eyes of the writer that picture floating in his inner self so that when you read this story you will understand the inspiration.

As I sat in the library taking a break from writing a research paper, I came across this picture which, in my opinion, captured the very essence of war in its truest form. So as I begin, the only thing I ask is that you open the eyes to your soul and see with your heart the devastation and brutality of war and how it transforms lives; how it takes little boys and turns them into killers with automatic weapons, how it takes grown men and turns them into angry, paranoid souls haunted by every image of death that is now seared into their subconscious; how the lack of soul and spirit rips away the virginity of innocent young girls. It became clear, as I gazed into this picture, that the brutality of war transforms the innocent into the vile and the vile into the lifeless. However, I asked myself this question: "Can innocence ever be regained after war leaves its indelible scar on the psyche of the soul?"

So for a moment, let me help you see what I saw as I gazed into that picture. In your mind's eyes, see a small European village close enough to the city that one would not call it rural but far enough away that one would not call it urban. It is a quiet little place with three-story inns, one school and, possibly, two churches. It is a place where excitement is the smell of home-cooked bread or pies resting in the windows of the village people. Now imagine seeing all those nice, quaint buildings demolished due to the relentless barrage of bombs falling from the sky, reducing the buildings to nothing more than piles of brick and mortar. As you look at the picture in your mind's eyes, see the sides of the buildings standing without any support like a wounded soldier resting on a crutch after battle, weak and tattered.

Now, see a group of children playing as though they were at the neighborhood park, totally oblivious of the absolute destruction surrounding them; see the smiles, joy, and excitement in the eyes of these children playing their favorite game as they run through the rubble and craters which are a reminder of the finality of war. As I looked at their faces, I asked myself, "How was this was possible that all seemed to have emotionally escaped the harrows of war?" But then I remembered the person in the forefront of the picture with his friends behind him, frolicking like deer in the forest. This little boy stood motionless. His gaze was mesmerizing as he looked right into the lens of the camera with big button eyes that were as empty as a hollow bell unable to sound its once beautiful tone. The difference between this little boy and the others was he was not running nor was he smiling. His stature was somewhat gaunt and frail as he slumped over his crutches, expressionless and emptied. As I looked at the two stories in one picture, I asked myself, "Which one was the real story of war?" Now I will leave that up to you.

Enjoy.

50

TWISTED SMILE

The devastation of war is shattering to most people looking at streets filled with debris from some bomb-shelled buildings, the roads spotted with unforgettable stains of red. But when there is nothing else except that in which you are engrossed, somehow the law of preservation sets in and it seems that people make do. It seems that children, the more innocent part of mankind, have a greater resilience than adults.

Looking at the faces of these youths, I do not see the ambivalence I would expect. Instead, their faces are filled with smiles, however fleeting that might be. Yet, somehow the faces of the others are inconsequential compared to the little boy in the forefront. His smile tells about a war that could only be seen through the eyes of a child. His smile tells of the pain from the loss of family and friends. A grimaced smile screams out about an irrevocable impairment suffered in a war he had nothing to do with. I see a forgivingness in his thin-lipped smirk of a smile that could only come from the heart of a child. As he stands there with a crutch under both arms, he looks at the others as they move about in a frolic he will never experience again. In the midst of all the bullet-ridden buildings and crumbled dreams, there can be hope. There can even be an amnesty through the twisted smile of a little boy.

ENDLESS WALK

Preface

Tupac Shakur referred to the streets as the "Thug Life." Once I placed that life behind me, two things chipped away at the old nature until I was unrecognizable by those who called themselves my hommies. It seemed finding God was one of the best decisions I had made as a young adult. The next was going back to school to do what I believed impossible— acquiring an education. Both of the above are transforming.

As I immersed myself in spirituality and knowledge, the world around me became my treasure chest, and I could not wait to get up to see where in the course of the day I would find my next gold coin. These golden coins were often tucked away in obscure places that challenged me spiritually and intellectually.

One afternoon, I learned the coins that I so diligently sought each day sometime came in the form of grace and mercy. One evening after being stimulated all day by the professors on the college campus, I began my long ride home on the bus. My mind was totally engrossed with information imparted by the wise ones called professors. As I stared out of the window, I could hear the bus driver calling out my street – 89th and Broadway. It seems my daydreaming prevented me from seeing the sun going down. I realized that after being detained by several instructors who took great pride in feeding my inquisitive mind, I lost track of time. I had been thrown off my game and as a result, must face the night. As I exited the bus, I realized it was dusk, and darkness seemed to fall all too fast with each passing step. My mind taunted me with

53

thoughts of my earlier life as a nocturnal perpetrator. Over the years I had become completely paranoid about being out after dark.

In the book of Job, there is one little verse that describes my feelings that night: "For the thing I greatly feared has come upon me, And what I dreaded has happened to me." (Job 3:25) For this reason, I knew it was going to be a long walk home this night, and the coins of God's grace and mercy would get me there.

Enjoy.

ENDLESS WALK

My grandfather once lived in the heart of a gang-infested neighborhood where walking down the street was like crossing the enemy line in a combat zone. You always expected the unexpected. While attending a local college in Los Angeles, I decided I would save gas by taking the bus from my grandfather's house to school. I was not thinking about the time or the distance I had to walk in the dark. Around 8:00 p.m., I found myself waiting for the back door of the bus to open. With beads of sweat sliding down my forehead and my heart sinking into my stomach, I suddenly realized that staying overtime, at school would come at the expense of my well-being. I stepped off the bus, having never seen this area before at night. I felt abandoned, as though for that moment the world had turned its back on me, and there would be no one to rescue me from my own bad decision.

I started to walk, but my steps seemed endless, as though I was gaining no ground. My paranoia grew with each step. I heard sirens piercing what I wished to be a calm and silent night. The occasional gun shots followed by screams did not help me much. I tried to increase my pace, but my legs were now moving without my control. The dogs barked in quadraphonic sound that night. Worst of all were the footstep—they came from everywhere, but when I turned to see, no one was there. I could see my grandfather's house, and somehow I knew that this night I would not become a casualty of the neighborhood war zone.

CHARLENE

Preface

While taking an advanced writing course as I moved toward earning another degree, the class studied the technique of descriptive writing through the works of such writers as Ernest Hemingway, Charles Dickens, and Edger Allen Poe. Our class held discussions on how the authors were able to capture the imagination of the reader without making the characters obvious. After several discussions, we were asked to put what we had learned to the test. Our teacher challenged us with an assignment that would truly test the very depths of our creativity and ability to conjure up images from our past. The instructor told the class to identify a person from our past and breathe life into them once again. This was a no-brainer for me because my character lived within the depths of my subconscious, forever seeking the opportunity to be set free. My goal was to take years of affiliation and reduce it into a couple of readable pages. At the same time, I knew I needed to introduce my character in such a subtle way that the character's complete identity would not be revealed until the end of the piece.

Once I started to write, words seemed to flow out of the ether. In the end, this image from my past was given life again, almost as complete and as clear as Lazarus rising from the dead and walking out of the tomb which held him captive. The analogy would be moving from the abyss of darkness to the exuberance of dawn. I became enthralled in my writing as this person whispered lost memories into my remembrance that I had long forgotten, and my pen gave them life once again.

Enjoy.

CHARLENE

To write this paper, I searched the depths of my subconscious mind and found a shadow of an image that I shall attempt to breathe life into once again. I found myself grabbing at any recollection of her that might spur my memory. I can almost see her in my mind's eye now.

She was somewhat tall for a woman, standing about five feet, eight inches. I thought she was rather willowy; others, from what I can recall, thought she was quite curvaceous. She had ivory-smooth skin, but ebony would probably describe her color best. She had very keen features – high cheek bones, very thin lips, and eyes that made you feel as though, when she looked at you, your whole life's story was being read. Her hair draped slightly above her shoulders and looked like ripples in the ocean when the wind blows.

Her voice was not the kind of voice you would expect from the coy and docile person she appeared to be. She had a kind of inflection in her voice that was almost haunting or maybe just a kind of quivering loneliness. When she smiled her whole body would light up with expression, but somehow happiness seemed to elude her. Her beauty, even though she did not flaunt it, was what she lived for. We sometimes selfishly think beauty is infinite but time waits for no one. As the experiences of life chipped away at her most prized possession, she became sullen, cutting off her communication with the world. As she sank deeper into her depression, I found myself oblivious to her plight.

I remember in junior high school, when my sensitivity was still somewhat untouched by a hardened world, this tall, willowy figure of a woman who had touched the very depth of my soul during the early years of my life, had reentered only to leave me once again.

It was the last week of school, and I had made plans to stop by and see her over the weekend. She had called me almost every day that week. Even though I had plenty of other calls coming in, I found myself waiting in great anticipation to talk to her. I was counting the days as they passed by. As my dad had to leave around mid-week, he hired someone to stay in the house with me while he was gone. I must have been plenty tired that Thursday, with only one more day to go. I came in from school and went right to bed, and sometime that evening she called. She asked to speak to me. The sitter told her I was asleep. She said with an even more haunting voice, "Tell him I love him." Then she hung up. That night she closed her eyes, never to open them again, and I never got a chance to say to her, "I love you." Somehow I think the maternal instinct of a mother transcended the silence of a son.

CHAMPAGNE IDEAS

Preface

This paper speaks to the rigors of writing that one research paper that challenges the very depth of your creativity. Often times the topic is given to the person by that well-intended professor who has more belief in your writing ability than you do. On this particular occasion, I was given one of those writing assignments by a professor I respected. I was told to write about writing, and I was told to explain my process of writing. First of all, I did not realize I had a process of writing until I sat down to write this paper. There is a lot we can learn in the process of writing. I once read a quote from an unknown author who said, "Anything written is twice thought." What a true statement, because through our writing we not only learn about the world around us, but we also learn about ourselves.

Writing has never come easy for me, so the thought of describing something that was in essence laborious, I knew it was going to be a challenge. How in the world do I write about writing? How do I take the topic of writing and turn it into a story that would hold the

interest of a reader? In this paper, I challenged myself to find the story as I described my process of writing.

Enjoy.

61

CHAMPAGNE IDEAS

Writing is somewhat of an arduous task for me. It never seems to come easy. Sometimes I write and write, and I never feel good about what I am writing. So I start over, and over, and over. Most of the time I start out writing about one thing and end up writing about something totally different.

All of my papers are written at my desk in my bedroom. It is a very old oak desk, given to me by my grandfather. Because of the size, it is sometimes a little cramped, with papers all over the top. Sometimes it looks like I am doing three or four assignments at once. But for some reason I seem to write better at my desk. I have tried writing at school and other places, but the ideas just do not come out when I am not at my desk. I have even tried going downstairs and writing at the kitchen table—nothing. Once I have an idea I try to organize the things I am going to write about, if not on paper, then in my mind. Once I have established some direction then I start my abuse of writing paper.

Now I am sitting down at my desk looking at the paper before my eyes. My mind is racing from one idea to another. I start to write, but inside my head it sounds like this, "How am I going to start this paper? What am I going to write about? Am I going to have enough to write about? Let me see if I can find a better word. I'd better check the spelling. I must not forget about the grammar. What am I going to place in the middle of this paper? How am I going to end now? I wonder if it makes sense? Maybe I'll get a good grade on this one. I do not like it. I think I'll start over." Then, just maybe I'll get that feeling. Yes, the feeling that tells me this is it.

Once I find something that feels good, the words just seem to come out endlessly. I guess you can say writing for me is a feeling from within that lets me know if I should keep going or stop and start again. One thing I have found is that when I get this feeling I cannot stop. I must sit and write until it is all out, like a cork being removed from a champagne bottle, and all the sparkling liquor pours out until there is none left. One might ask, "What about tomorrow?" Hopefully I will be able to find another bottle of champagne.

THE GREATNESS OF LIFE

Preface

Late one night about 30 years ago I watched an old movie in black and white. The premise of the movie was a battle between good and evil, light and dark. Towards the end of the movie, the protagonist looked up as though he was speaking directly to me. I stared at the television, motionless, waiting to hear what this man had to say to me. As we looked one another in the eyes, he said, "Is there a love greater than an illusion and stronger than the shadows of death?" My mouth dropped because this question almost caused me to burn a fuse; it was too much to take in at one time or at one sitting. I held on to this statement as I slept that night and pondered it throughout the greater part of the next day until I felt compelled and inspired to write. This is a synopsis of the essence of the movie—pitting evil against good, light against darkness, and love against death.

Enjoy.

THE GREATNESS OF LIFE

While pondering something I had heard one day, I fell off into a deep sleep. While in my slumber, two images slowly manifested on either side of me. As I watched them reach the point of total manifestation, a warmth and comfort caressed my right side. I stood in great silence, then the silence was broken. The being to my right began to speak. He said, "I am life. I am the Alpha and the Omega. I am the beginning and the end. I am life. I am the joy of a day within a day that makes a day. I am the radiant feeling of comfort when disillusion tries to get in. I am life. I am that which is good. I am the sun that pierces down with warmth and warms you in the day. I am the joy of life."

As he spoke, a cool breeze suddenly moved across my body toward my right side and a voice followed with a deep, melancholy tone and a cynical smirk of pompous arrogance, "I am death. I am the darkness of dark. I am the prince of nothingness. I am death, and where I reign there is no light. I am the darkness that one enters." He went on with great boastful pride to say, "In my darkness there is sadness. In my darkness there is a comfort." And at that moment the light to my right became brighter than ever, interjecting with the peaceful authority of raging waters, saying, "There is no comfort in death and there is no truth in darkness for I am life and life is before death, for I am the beginning and I shall be the end. Death shall never prevail above life nor will bad against good. I am life. I am that I am."

Suddenly I began to remember the question I pondered so deeply: "Is there a love greater than illusion and stronger than the shadows of death?" There is a love greater than illusion and stronger than the shadows of death. Yes, there is a love greater than illusion and stronger than the shadows of death. As I found myself repeating this over and over again, there was a joy and peace that entered my inner-being. I looked to my right and the image of life was fading. He said, "Life shall prevail, for more human existence is life, be it the will to survive, the pursuit of happiness, or life itself."

BLACK LIKE ME

Preface

While working on a degree in psychology at the local community college, I wrote this piece. I remember it clearly because it was around the time of the L. A. riots. Within a short period of time, I believe I went from being accepted as an African-American person laboring to be accepted in the world of academia, but treated as an outcast ostracized by the Caucasian community on campus because of the color of my skin. I was looked down on like I was a member of an anti-government group screaming "Let's overtake the establishment." The sad thing was, this was the last place I would have expected to be treated like an outcast because of my race.

As an idealist, I believed an institution of higher learning was where minds were challenged to think outside of the box, ask questions, and dare to be different. I believed this institution was where people were being pushed outside their comfort zones formed by culture, family, and society. I believed the quest for knowledge forced people to see situations once viewed superficially, in-depth and scholarly. Well, I was wrong, because the same kind of bigotry I experienced on the outside of the campus, by people who were not striving to become educators, scholars, mathematicians, or scientist, was now on the inside with the same intensity of hatred and lack of understanding.

My honors English instructor had given our class an assignment, and I chose to allow my disappointment to be expressed through this assignment. I did not know how it was going to happen. I just knew that if I were successful, I would have something special. I began to write.

After finishing my draft, I headed over to the student learning center where I could have my paper proofed. It seemed the inconvenience of being dyslexic kept me depending on others to be my second set of eyes. So I headed off to the student learning center to have my paper proofed by a professor during his or her down time on campus. I stood in line and began to wait my turn to spend time with the acting professor of the hour.

As I waited, it became clear that my rich brown presence and the present disruption in the African-American community had a profound impact on the people around me, including the acting professor whom I would present my paper to. The professor periodically glanced up at me as if to say to himself, "He is still there." Have you ever felt someone's eyes cut across you and felt the disdain they have for you? It was as though my very presence repulsed this man, and all this was said before I ever sat with him face to face. In spite of the unspoken negative energy I felt exuding from this person, I waited until my turn came to present my work. The man looked at me and immediately snatched the paper out of my hand, grabbed his red pen and instantly started making violent strokes across my paper with his pen until he paused long enough to read the contents. It took a few seconds for the man to release his red sword that violently ripped through the first part of my paper, and I watched his demeanor go through a complete metamorphosis, showing a myriad of emotions from disdain, blame, and fear to shame. At this point, still reading, he appeared to be savoring every word on the paper. Now at the end of his reading, the paper was given back with fewer red marks than I anticipated.

The bible reads that the eyes are the windows to the soul, and if this is the case, his eyes were filled with remorse, shame, and the apology I knew he would never verbalize. It does not matter because I know "The pen is mightier than the sword."

Enjoy.

Black Like Me

Describing something I have experienced all my life will not be too difficult. First of all, I am identified by a color that does not come close to describing the rich brown pigmentation I was born with. Sometimes I am looked upon, stared at, hated, and even feared without ever opening my mouth. People have these reactions all because of the color black. In today's society of education and high technology, I ponder the question, "How long will black and I be synonymous with one another?"

I have heard people say that if a black cat crosses your path, you will have bad luck. Black is the sightless night that people fear. Black is the crow that farmers hate because they leave little for the yearly harvest. Black is the spider people walk around for fear of its bite. Black is the race of indigenous people from a far-away land. Black is the day of satanic worshiping better known as Black Sabbath. Black is the so-called color of a people with kinky hair, wide noses, thick lips, illiterate by nature and always on the verge of violence. Black is a minority from birth to death, no matter how many degrees one obtains or how far one climbs the economic ladder of success. Black is the color so rich and so pure, its depth is like the word infinity, "never ending or beginning."

Yes, I have answered to this color that I am not, and it is time to dispel the myth. I am not illiterate nor am I a degenerate. I am not a devil worshiper nor would I destroy the crop of a laborious farmer. I do not consider myself a virulent creature waiting to strike someone. I am as mystified of the dark as anyone else. If black is a color, then allow me to introduce myself as something other than a color with a negative connotation. I am a person, a person who bleeds and has compassion and feelings, who seeks love from a world filled with stereotypes and stigmas. I am a being, not a color. If black is a color, then when I am looked upon, do not stop until you see the truth of my essence.

Let us, as modern-day beings, work collectively to dispel the myths of racism, hatred, prejudice, and stereotypes. I understand that will probably not happen in my lifetime, so maybe one day I will learn not to answer when someone identifies and associates me with the color with a negative connotation. If only when people look upon me they could see the beauty of the spirit within and not the color of the exterior. Let us judge one another on the basis of our character, not color. If we must color one another, let us always keep in mind the splendor in the sky after every rain, and maybe, as a people, we can hold hands while searching for that pot of gold called life.

THE VISION TO REACH NATIONS FOR GOD

Preface

Sometimes in our worst state, God is attempting to birth something new and different in us. After three bouts with an illness I could not shake, I found myself in the hospital, in and out of consciousness, struggling for clarity and understanding, and I remember asking God this question: "Why me Lord?" For several days, when I was not over taken by the severe pain which paralyzed my body and mind, I would ask God this question: "Why me Lord?" I clearly remember my argument to defend my position with God; it sounded something like this:

I do not smoke.
I do not drink.
I do not curse.
I am not having an affair.
I am a good parent who loves his children.
I do not do drugs.
I am a responsible husband.

"Why me?" For several days, while grappling with my mortality, I received no response or relief from God. Feeling that God had turned His back on me in my time of desperation, I changed my question of humble submission to "What are you trying to teach me Lord?" At that moment, I realized the arrogance of the question I had been asking God. You see, every time I asked God "Why me?," I was telling Him I was too good to endure the testing of this life. I was too holy to be tried and too righteous to stand on the front line with those under

73

fire. With the tender spirit of an afternoon breeze caressing one's face ever so gingerly, God whispered in my spirit: "Why not you?" It seemed from this point on the loving mercy of God cradled my broken soul like the arms of a mother who needed her child to know they were going to be alright.

I spent two more weeks in the hospital, not in pain, but in consultation with my heavenly father who ministered to me physically, mentally, and spiritually. As I regained my strength, it became clear that I had lost my focus to reach nations for Christ. I had settled for a church and an altar that caused me to focus only on those on the inside and not those on the outside. God was sharing with me that the real church was not confined to four walls but was wherever two or more gathered. I had been in church all my life, but it was at this point that I truly found church.

Enjoy.

THE VISION TO REACH NATIONS FOR GOD

In sharing my testimony of how God has given me a vision for mission, there are three main points and two scriptures that have changed my life forever. These points and scriptures are listed below. My prayer for those of you who read this testimony is that your life may be convicted, challenged, and enriched by the words of this avowal:

- **Daring to dream**
- **Discovering your passion**
- **Walking by faith**

Psalms 46:10: Be still, and know that I am God; I will be exalted among the nation; I will be exalted in the earth!

☐ <u>Daring to Dream</u>

Let me share a little about how this scripture spoke to me in the midst of a great storm in my life. Many times as a pastor I have heard the Voice of God speaking to me, but I was too busy tending the sheep to listen. In the "all too interesting" paradox of life, it seems that I, the one who should have been talking to God the most, found myself in a place where I had put God on hold. But what I have come to understand is that God will only remain on hold for so long, and that no one wants to be left holding the phone when God hangs up.

This is not because God is going to pour out the wrath of Hell Fire and Brimstone on us when we leave Him on hold, but it is in these moments that we come into an understanding of just how frail we are without JEHOVAH-RAAH (the Lord, my Shepherd and Protector).

***Psalms 102:2* reads: *Hide not thy face from me in the day
when I am in trouble; incline thine ear unto me; in the day
when I call, answer me speedily.***

Sometimes circumstances have to render us immobile in order
for God to get our full attention. In January 2003, I was stricken
by three attacks of a severe case of pancreatitis. The third
attack left me in the hospital flat on my back for two weeks.

It was during the first and second attacks that I found myself
asking God that age-old question: "Why me Lord?" And the more
I asked God "why," the more frustrated I became because there
was no response on the other end of the line. Unable to move
and in too much pain to talk, I was forced to just be still and know
that He was God. By the time I experienced my third attack, I
changed my question and it sounded something like this: "Okay,
Lord, you have my attention. What are you trying to tell me?"

☐ **Discovering Our Passion Can Be Like Finding Hidden Treasure**

Judges 14:6-9

I heard a great man of God speak on these verses, and
he summed them up like this: "Out of the struggle comes
something sweet."

In the throes of my struggles, I felt God was asking me
where was my passion for the Kingdom. Of course, I responded
to God with the thing I was most comfortable with in my life,
pastoring a Church. Over the years, I have accepted pastoring
as my one and only true passion, but somehow I felt God was
challenging me to go deeper. And deeper I went until I found
a hidden passion for mission work that I had buried in fear,
doubt, and lack of faith. I, like most people, had gravitated
toward the things in my life that came easiest for me. I knew
in my spirit that mission work for the Lord meant dedication,
sacrifice, and moving out on faith.

76

Even though I had exercised these things while pastoring, I knew in my heart that mission work would cause me to reach deeper into my walk of faith. I found myself questioning the Lord, asking Him if I was ready to do the work of an evangelist/ missionary. I realized when you are thousands of miles away from home, family, friends, and your comfort zone, God becomes an absolute source of strength, and faith is not an option.

With so many convenient crutches in my life, running from my passion was relatively easy. It then dawned on me that in my state of spiritual complacency, I had not only refused to change, but I had jeopardized my own growth as a Christian by keeping God on hold.

- **Hospital Room Monologue versus Dialogue**

Once I stopped asking God why, the pity party monologue of a prayer stopped and a wonderful dialogue of communion filled my spirit as I laid there in the hospital. The hold button was off, and I could hear a familiar voice on the other end saying, "I love you, and I have been waiting for you for some time." We talked about all the important things He had been trying to share with me while He was on hold.

I had almost forgotten what it felt like being in the loving presence of God because most of my time through counseling and pastoring was spent helping others get there. With so much expected of me while pastoring, I learned to give of myself unconditionally, but found I had cheated God, family and friends when it came to receiving.

For two weeks, I lived on the strongest pain medicine the hospital had to offer. My communication with God took place while waiting to be medicated or praying to sleep away the pain. As my body healed, God started sharing with me how He wanted to change my path. For twenty-some years, the call of pastoring a church has been my life's mission, and now

God was changing my course.   I asked why and I asked how, but in the end, I said to the Lord, "Here am I, send me." I did not care about the path I was being challenged to walk anymore as long as the Lord was on the other end of the line.

My trial had led up to this moment of receiving a vision from God for a ministry that would reach the world with the Gospel of Jesus Christ, and I trembled in my shoes. I have never considered myself a great preacher or evangelist, and now God was calling me to reach nations for the Kingdom. I found myself feeling like Moses when he decided to remind God of his inadequacies, but God reminded Moses that all sufficiency for human existence rested within the great "I am." Moses did not understand the gift and the calling. You see, when God called Moses, He had already gifted him with what he needed to do the job. I, too, like Moses, found myself relying on the great "I am" for guidance and direction.

☐   **Learning How to Walk by Faith**

II Corinthians 5:7: For we walk by faith, not by sight.

It has become increasingly clear that if I am to proceed with creating an international ministry from scratch, it will only happen by me walking by faith and not by sight. I have preached faith from the pulpit to the hospital rooms, but now God was challenging me to walk in every word I had preached over the years.

Every day I am reminded that accepting this call to reach nations for God, teaching, empowering, and saving souls is summed up best in this verse found in *Zechariah 4:6: Not by might, nor by power, but by my Spirit, saith the Lord of host.*

METAMORPHOSIS OF A SOUL

Preface

There is an old saying that goes something like this: We all have skeletons in our closets. The interesting thing about this statement is I have never heard anyone say where these skeletons come from or how we acquire them. What became increasingly clear to me is, wherever these skeletons come from, they represent past behaviors and deeds. It took years of maturing and experiencing life to acquire some of the skeletons that I placed in my closet.

As children, we tend to be transparent living up to another old saying: What you see is what you get. But as adults, we quickly learn how to blend in by identifying with those things around us that are socially acceptable. So then, what do we do with the remnants of our past behaviors, deeds, and stories that may not be socially accepted? If you are like me, you tucked those skeletons away, for it is far more important to be accepted in superficiality than in blatant honesty.

It seems these suppressed thoughts behind closed doors over a period of time start to resemble skeletons—dried, withered, and lifeless. My reality came when I realized the harder I tried to conceal these skeletons from the world around me the more I found myself reflecting that which I hid from the world. At some point, I began to question who was really locked behind the closed door that shielded the world from my past. Now feeling enslaved by my secrets or the skeletons locked away in my closet, I became overwhelmingly disconsolate. For some reason, I believed I would be castigated by the moral and ethical judgment of those around me if I told the truth.

Freedom comes through many avenues and often when least expected. One day, while in an advanced writing class, I was challenged by an assignment to connect with the skeletons in my closet. The question we were asked was "What would they say if they had the opportunity to speak?" I wrestled with the duality of my thoughts—do I hold on to them or do I let them go? Ultimately, I embraced this challenge like a hopeless man seeing light at the end of a tunnel for the first time.

Enamored at the thought of freedom, I began to write, even at the risk of exposing my skeletons, and with each stroke of the pen, I felt the door open wider and wider. After hours and hours of writing, I emerged from my cocoon determined to no longer be defined by my past but strengthened.

Now looking back in retrospect I believe my journey came down to this, the freedom I sought could only come from me facing the skeletons in my closet, not hiding them away. In this piece, I became the butterfly emerging from the dark confines of limitation into the sunlit daybreak of freedom and opportunity.

Enjoy.

METAMORPHOSIS OF A SOUL

This entire allegory, I said, you may now append, dear Glaucon, to the previous argument; the prison-house is the world of sight, the light of the fire is the sun, and you will not misapprehend me if you interpret the journey upwards to be the ascent of the soul into the intellectual world according to my poor belief, which, at your desire, I have expressed—whether rightly or wrongly God knows. But, whether true or false, my opinion is that in the world of knowledge the idea of good appears last of all, and is seen only with an effort; and, when seen, is also inferred to be the universal author of all things beautiful and right, parent of light and of the lord of light in this visible world, and the immediate source of reason and truth in the intellectual; and that this is the power upon which he who would act rationally, either in public or private life must have his eye fixed. (Plato, *The Republic: Allegory of the Cave*, 380 B.C.)

An intellectual climb from the depth of darkness to the exuberance of daylight can best describe my ascent from the cave which held me captive for so long. The dark morose cave which I dwelt in for so long became my reality. The images, however twisted and disfigured, were all that I had.

From the age of six to eighteen, the streets of South Central Los Angeles were my cave, and illiteracy was the chain which held me bound. I blamed my servitude on the world around me, never thinking to look within myself. At around age seven, it became quite clear to me that we were poor and that there were only two kinds of people in the world—those who have and those who have not.

Unemployment ran rampant in my community, along with a fifty-cent bottle of wine called Ripple for the men on the corner to obliterate the reality of not being able to provide for their families. The youth walked up and down the streets with no particular destination in mind, always being very careful not to cross the neighborhood boundaries for fear of surprise attacks from the other youths out walking with nowhere to go. Fights and robberies were all too frequent. Death was something we learned and accepted at a very young age.

I soon grew old enough to join the fellows walking up and down the streets. We would meet each day around the corner or in front of someone's house, remain there until we were asked to leave, then we would start our aimless walks. Once we all got together, things just seemed to happen. Though never really planned, we were just a group of young men with nowhere to go. I soon discovered a quality I possessed called leadership. For some reason, the fellows looked to me for direction, and direct them I did. Like a wild animal pacing back and forth in a cage, I became restless with all the boundaries closing in on me. I started taking my followers into other territories. This brought some excitement into our lives; to us it was no more than a game. Our lives became the objects of chance and dare. Some of us were shot, some were stabbed, and some were beaten beyond recognition. Some were even laid to rest with the gang colors across their chest. We soon conquered all the surrounding areas and would strut from block to block like peacocks basking in our victory, power, and control.

Again I found myself restless and needed something else to challenge me, so I began an operation of distributing drugs. I did not realize this was just another shadow on the wall of the cave, another distortion of reality which helped me justify my actions. For me, the selling of drugs took me out of poverty and placed me among those who have in America.

One day a good friend purchased some of my commodities, and a couple days later someone told me this friend was in the hospital close to death due to a drug overdose. I started thinking that if I really cared for my friend as I said I did, then I would not have sold him drugs. I took a good look at what drugs were doing to the community in which I lived. Most of my friends were dead or strung out on drugs. It was time for me to make a change.

I kept my business going for a little while longer, but during this time I started to read books. I guess you could say this was the first time I realized there was more to life than the distorted images on the wall in my cave. I read books about Dr. Martin Luther King, Jr., Harriet Tubman, Frederick Douglass, Thurgood Marshall, and Malcolm X. The more I read, the more I wanted to know about the world around me.

My appetite for reading literature on Black History soon could only be described in one word, voracious. From my reading, I learned words like degenerate, servitude and genocide. For a person who had never graduated from high school, I suddenly found myself speaking on issues I would have normally been ignorant of.

After severing all ties with my *underground* business, I emerged on the college campus of El Camino in Torrance, California. This was my reality of light outside the cave. How precious this light was to me in all of its infinite wisdom. The shadow that followed me was no longer contorted but erect and clear. I found a new world of knowledgeable people who spoke about elevating their consciousness and changing the direction of the world through politics. I found myself becoming a part of the system I had fought so long and hard against. I assimilated this knowledge like a delectable meal.

Now strengthened by the freedom and wisdom of the light outside the cave, I decided it was time to go back and tell the people who supported my underground life about my amazing discovery. I went back to my old community and stopped first at the house where we used to hang out. It did not take long for the word to get around that I was back.

Those who had once been followers came to see me, but they only stared with a smirk of disgust on their faces. My dress, my walk, and my speech had changed; somehow the light had made me almost unrecognizable. With an excitement, I told them anyway about the light outside the cave and that the shadows on the wall were only reflections of beautiful objects just on the other side.

Now saddened because the darkness had limited their ability to see beyond the walls of their caves, they said it was too far out of their reach, and the shadows on their walls were all they had. At this point, I realized I had been ostracized from the people and community I had once been a part of because of the light. My stay after that was brief because the light outside was beckoning my presence. I knew I could never be a part of the cave of darkness as long as there was light.

BLACK AND BROWN LIVES DO MATTER

Preface

This is an excerpt from a speech I gave at a Black Lives Matter rally in Indio, California. I was deeply concerned about what I had to say and how it might offend those in attendance: members of the local police department for their courageous service rendered to the community, the Hispanic community grieving over the loss of family and community members assaulted by those with gang-member mentalities in uniform, and the African-American community which at that time was grieving over a history of losses at the hands of those empowered by a badge, uniform, and gun. So after days of trepidation and deliberation, I decided to just walk in my truth and simply share the narrative from my own personal perspective. At this point, I figured no matter what I said someone would disagree and find reason to be offended.

Enjoy

BLACK AND BROWN LIVES DO MATTER

I have been asked to say a few words about why we are gathered here this evening. I believe I was asked not because I am the most articulate speaker in the valley or, for that matter, a charismatic pastor, but because those spearheading this event knew I would be sensitive, honest, forthright, and loving as I approached a very challenging subject that is now ripping at the hearts of Americans across our great nation.

My name is Dr. Tahlib McMicheaux. I am the pastor of a local church in Desert Hot Springs, California. Today we gather as a collective body representing humanity with a conscience. This collective body of humanity tells us there is still hope. We gather because our disappointment has not become hopelessness. We gather as realists seeking the opportunity to become idealists.

This epidemic we call "Policing in America" is claiming a life within the black and brown community every 36 hours. We gather because there is a fierce urgency, and our nation needs to respond expeditiously. Today we are asking our legislators across our nation to stand still long enough to hear the voices of our youth crying out from the stained pavements across our nation. The blood of our youth has been given a voice, and it is asking for justice and vengeance. The voices of our children have reached the heart of our Creator who looks down in shame at His creation. He is asking those empowered, "What have you done to your brother?"

I believe the heart of God is grieved by the retort of those empowered saying, "Am I my brother's keeper?" (Genesis 4:9.) The arrogance of this statement solidifies the unequal playing field in America for millions of people of color. Those empowered are not concerned about their children not coming home from a trip to the grocery store or a drive to a friend's house. Their response lets us know there is a group of people in America that has received their inoculations, freeing them from the devastation of this epidemic of violence.

This epidemic is now causing the citizens of our great nation to question whether the scales of justice need to be recalibrated, for the pendulum appears to be stuck on one side.

This epidemic has gained the attention of people around the world who are now looking to see how long America is going to allow this plague to devastate communities before she oils the pendulum of justice that is failing millions of people of color. The world is looking on in awe at the disproportionate rate of black and brown lives that are being imprisoned and jailed through mass incarceration. The world is looking on in astonishment at the failed attempts to address societal needs where America creates laws that solely govern the black and brown community.

We are asking today: How long will America allow this epidemic to devastate our communities? How long will she allow the world to look on from the outside, gasping at the injustices and fatalities? How long before America, the superpower, stops rescuing third-world countries and begins the greatest humanitarian rescue of the 21st century? When will she begin to rescue her own black and brown lives within the inner cities from those who are operating with a militia mentality? How long before we stop singing *Kumbaya* and *We Shall Overcome* and become a nation with a conscience, compelled to live out the words of Dr. Martin Luther King, Jr., "Injustice anywhere is a threat to justice everywhere"? (*Letter*

From Birmingham Jail, April 16, 1963, p1.) How long before the silent majority establishes an equal playing field that restores dignity to all American citizens regardless of color, creed, or nationality? Yes, the playing field is not equal, and the epidemic, if left alone, will shortly become a pandemic threat to the longevity of all people of color in America.

We are here as the moral conscience of America to remind her that the voices of those slain are screaming from the blood-stained streets throughout our nation. We are here today to remember those whose lives were claimed by this devastating epidemic:

- Michael Brown,
- Trayvon Martin,
- Danny Rodriguez,
- Oscar Grant,
- John Crawford,
- Ezell Ford,
- Dante Parker,
- and Erick Garner, to name a few.

We are also here to bring attention to the injustices and inequities within our judicial system. We are here to say that bigotry, prejudice, racial profiling, and the abuse of power within agencies sworn to serve and protect the American citizen, regardless of socioeconomic status, color, or creed, must end.

I believe there are some "suited in blue" who are conducting themselves as though they are members of a college fraternity, sworn to secrecy, forgetting their public oath to the people they vowed to serve. They are the ones who have become agents of death, carrying this epidemic of violence that is devastating our communities. Having said that, let me say this, "I want it to be known that I do not believe all who wear the blue uniform are abusing their power." However, the Bible reads, "A little bit of leaven spoils the whole lump." (Galatians 5:9.) It is a few that are causing the whole to look bad, and it is for this reason we must act swiftly in righting the injustices of those who have made spreading this epidemic their life's mission.

We are here to say that we, as a people, need the pendulum of justice to swing equally toward the blue fraternity as well as our minority communities, for justice cannot be justice if it is partial to either side. The world is watching our judicial system which up to now has shown favoritism and partiality toward those empowered, while the gavel of justice releases its fury enforcing the three-strikes law on the minority community throughout our nation.

We have come together as a people of faith and a community of believers asking our nation to release the cure for this epidemic. We have gathered here to demand that the halls of justice in America release the antidote to remedy this outbreak that has devastated our communities. The antidote for this epidemic is justice and equality **for all**, not just for those empowered and those who are abusing their power.

We believe our congress, senators, and lawmakers are holding back on releasing the antidote. Today we are asking our congress, senators, and legislators to listen to the voices of those whose blood has stained the streets across our communities, crying out for justice and vindication. We are asking that you hear the weeping mothers and fathers across America who are going to bed without their child because this plague of violence has claimed yet another life.

We need our legislators, today, to stop talking about designated, earmarked money that has been set aside for body cameras. We need the authorities to release that funding so our judicial system will have more than one perspective when reviewing these fatalities in our communities. We need our legislators and policymakers to take this epidemic seriously and make it a priority. Today it is our children, but tomorrow it could be yours. You can only remain immune to this epidemic for so long. We need our legislators to reach into the vaults of the great halls of justice and bring out the antidote that will save millions of lives that have only started to live.

And lastly, I would like to speak to the pastors, community leaders, and parents. The arrogance of our enemy has exposed him for who he is, a bully and a parasite who lives on everyone else's blood. We must realize that even though we are no longer fighting desegregation or the ills of Jim Crow, our 21st century battle to eradicate an epidemic that thrives on de facto discrimination must be fought with the same ferocity as of old. Therefore, as leaders, we must understand it is our responsibility to educate our black and brown young men and women on how to contain their youthful exuberance when confronted by law enforcement, for it appears this exuberance is often misinterpreted as a form of militancy and defiance.

So today we fight the justification of a dominant society that refuses to see or treat people of color as equals. We fight the ills of capitalism and free enterprise that led to the enslavement of over 4 four million Africans because of the color of their skin.

Yes, we scream **Black Lives Matter** because white lives did not come to America in chains. We scream **Black Lives Matter** because laws were not created to take away the rights of white America but to give them more rights. We scream **Black Lives Matter** because white lives did not have to sit at the back of the bus. We scream **Black Lives Matter** because black people did not put on white sheets to lynch white Americans. We scream **Black Lives Matter** because of the disproportionate rate at which black lives are claimed daily by this epidemic violence that is sweeping our nation. We scream **Black Lives Matter** because we are listening to the voices of those whose blood has stained the streets of America crying out for justice and vindication.

Tonight, let us light candles because our nation has gone dark, because city halls across America have gone dark, because our nation's capital has gone dark, and because the White House, with all its brilliance, has gone dark. These buildings that are supposed to represent the people of America have gone dark because they have failed to stand up for the people; they have refused to listen to the voices of those slain; they refuse to hear the weeping parents; and they refuse to release the antidote.

We are asking every concerned American of all colors and nationalities to demand that our local and national leaders release the antidote for this epidemic of violence. This antidote is an equal playing field that provides people of color with equitable rights, justice, and equality.

There is a small book in the Bible called *Amos* with a little verse that sums up our struggle: "But let justice roll down like waters, and righteousness like an ever-flowing stream." (Amos 5:24.) We want what America has failed to give us for over 400 years – justice, justice, justice, and justice.

Made in the USA
Las Vegas, NV
20 January 2025